FACT FINDERS

Educational adviser: Arthur Razzell

Clothes and Ornaments

Stephanie Thompson

Illustrated by John Sibbick,
Richard Hook and Dick Eastland
Designed by Faulkner/Marks Partnership

Macmillan Education Limited

©1976 Macmillan Education Limited

Published in the United
States by Silver Burdett
Company, Morristown, N.J.
1978 Printing

ISBN 0-382-06239-6

Library of Congress
Catalog Card No. 78-64657

Clothes and Ornaments

National Costume

Today, many people in different countries wear the same kinds of clothes. But on special occasions they sometimes wear national costume. National costumes are often colourful, like these Russian ones (right).

Nigeria

**Germany
(Black Forest)**

At one time, national costumes were people's everyday clothes. In some countries, they are still quite common.

Many Japanese people, for example, still wear the *Kimono* (left).

Tibet

Argentina
(Gaucho)

New Zealand
(Maori)

The First Clothes

The first men and women wore no clothes at all. The earliest clothes were made out of animal skins (left). People also made clothing from plants.

Fiji warriors (below) still sometimes wear grass skirts.

Cro-Magnon man

The Ancient Egyptians were the first people to weave cloth to make clothes. In the Middle East, women still weave cloth on ground looms (below).

Navajo Indians (right) are famous for their hand-woven cloth.

Ground loom

As time went by, dress became more decorative.

The Ancient Egyptians dyed cloth to make bright colours (left). They used bone needles to sew pieces of cloth together. They also made jewellery, such as necklaces and rings.

The Chinese were the first people to weave silk (below).

Chinese ladies of the 6th century

Senator's wife

Senator

Fashionably-dressed lady

Workman

In Ancient Rome, clothes showed a person's importance in society.

Only Roman citizens could wear long robes called togas. A Senator wore a purple stripe on his toga.

A thousand years after the Romans, dress still showed people's importance. The dress of ordinary people was very simple. You can see what it looked like from this painting of a wedding, below.

Kings and queens, and other important people wore rich clothes. They also wore fine jewellery.

Queen Elizabeth 1

Lady

Rich people spent a lot of money on clothes. Men were just as interested in clothes and jewels as women were.

Sleeves and breeches were often slashed to show fine lining material.

EUROPEAN DRESS, 16th CENTURY

Tailor

Gentleman

Modern Clothes

Day clothes 1805

Fashions in clothes often seem to repeat themselves. In the Regency period in England, men wore rich clothes (left). In Victorian times, dark suits became the fashion. The photograph (above) shows a Victorian family.

1900 **1910** **1920**

In our own century, there have been many different fashions. You can see some of them at the top of this page.

Present-day fashions are for the sort of comfortable clothes shown in the photograph (right).

Clothes for Work

Many people wear special clothes for work. People who have dangerous jobs wear protective clothing. The welder (below left) shields his face with a mask.

People working with drugs (right) wear sterilised clothes.

Welder, wearing mask

Scuba divers, Australia

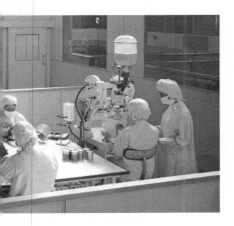

Astronauts (below), firemen and frogmen all need special clothes for protection.

In some jobs, people wear uniforms so that they are easily recognised. This is why a policeman wears a uniform, for instance.

Astronauts wearing spacesuits

Special clothes are worn for many sports. In team games, different teams wear different colours.

American footballers (below) wear protective padded clothing. Fencers (right) wear masks.

Skiers (opposite) wear warm, waterproof clothing. They also have strong boots, gloves and goggles.

Fencing

American football

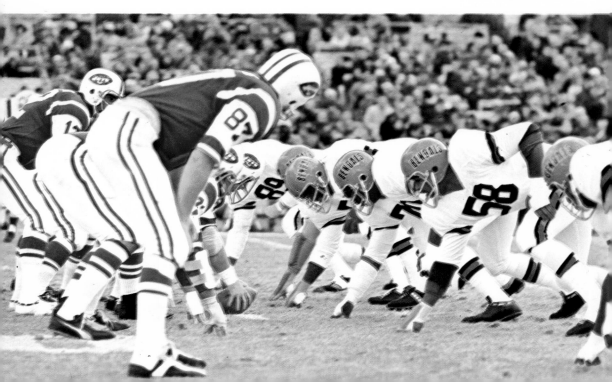

Skiing

Clothes in War

German armour, 17th century

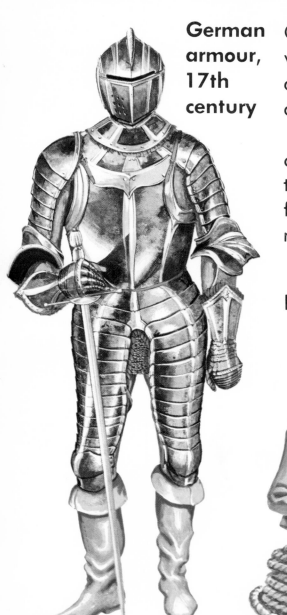

Clothes for war have changed as warfare itself has changed. Long ago, knights wore suits of steel armour like the one on the left.

At one time, sailors wore their own clothes. When these wore out, they were replaced by spare clothes from the ship. This became the first naval uniform.

Naval dress

1885

1799

Today

French Hussar 1807

Many years ago soldiers wore brightly coloured uniforms. This French trooper (left) had a helmet which made him look taller.

Modern soldiers (below) wear uniforms that do not show up well. This kind of 'disguise' is called camouflage.

Ceremonial dress is often based on uniforms of the past. On the left is a French Republican guard. In England, Beefeaters still guard the Tower of London.

The Swiss Guard is the Pope's personal bodyguard.

English Beefeater

Swiss Guard

Other people wear ceremonial costume on special occasions only. When a king or queen is crowned, they wear special robes.

The Nigerian horseman shown here is wearing an elaborate ceremonial costume.

Glossary

Armour   Any covering that protects a man in battle.

Astronaut   A person who travels into space.

Breeches   Old-fashioned tight trousers, usually fastened below the knee.

Camouflage   Disguise which makes the wearer hard to see.

Jewellery   Ornaments worn for personal decoration. Jewellery includes rings, bracelets and necklaces.

Kimono   Loose Japanese robe with wide sleeves, held at the waist with a sash.

Knight   Medieval soldier, usually of high birth.

Loom   Machine used for weaving thread into cloth.

Protective clothing   A form of dress designed to protect its wearer from danger or discomfort.

Senator   A member of the council which ruled Ancient Rome. Today the name is used in some countries to describe a member of a governing body.

Silk   Fine cloth made from the thread spun by the worms of the silkworm moth.

Uniform   Special clothing worn by a particular group of people such as policemen and firemen. Some schools have a uniform which all their pupils wear.

Welder   Person who joins pieces of metal together. He often does this by heating the metal with a special tool.

1 2 3 4 5 6 7 8 9 10— R —85 84 83 82 81 80 79